The Census 1801-1911

A GUIDE FOR THE INTERNET ERA

Stuart A. Raymond

THE FAMILY HISTORY PARTNERSHIP

Published by
The Family History Partnership
PO Box 502
Bury, Lancashire BL8 9EP
Webpage: www.familyhistorypartnership.co.uk
Email: sales@thefamilyhistorypartnership.com

in association with
S.A. & M.J. Raymond
Webpage: www.stuartraymond.co.uk
Email: samjraymond@btopenworld.com

ISBNs:
Family History Partnership: 978 1 906280 16 1
S.A. & M.J. Raymond: 978 1 899688 53 3

First Published 2009

Printed and bound by
Information Press. Southfield Road, Eynsham
Oxford OX29 4JB

Contents

Acknowledgements

I am grateful to Sue Lumas, Richard Ratcliffe, and Brett Langston, who have all commented on drafts of this book. Richard provided the information on the Ratcliffe family used for case study 2. I am grateful too to Bob Boyd, who has seen it through the press. Crown copyright in official census documents reproduced here is acknowledged.

Introduction

The aim of this book is to provide basic information about the census for both family and local historians: how and when it was compiled, what information it provides, where it can be consulted, and how to use it. Family and local historians share a common interest in the census. They have an advantage over other historians, since they are likely to possess a good knowledge of local topography, and know where particular houses actually were in relation to others. Local and family historians need, however, to be more aware of the various purposes for which the census can be used.

Census enumerators' books (sometimes referred to as census returns) are vital sources of information for all social and economic historians interested in the Victorian period. The editor of the *Illustrated London news* was absolutely right when he wrote in 1851 that 'the numbering of the people at regular intervals is a duty which the people owe to themselves, and to the generations that are to follow them'. The census can be used to study a particular family, or to undertake a total history of a particular street or parish. It is also possible to use it for regional or national studies of subjects such as the disappearance of servants, or the process of urbanisation.

The official census enumerators' books are only available from 1841 until 1911 at present. Earlier returns have been destroyed, although some unofficial name lists are available for family historians, and the official census reports are invaluable for local historians.

Who were the members of a particular family? That is one of the basic questions that family historians seek to answer. The census provides much of the information needed. For the period it covers, it offers a decennial listing of the resident members of every family recorded, and may provide information which is unavailable elsewhere. From 1851, it reveals the relationships of heads of households towards other members. The development of internet databases means that we can now instantly search the census for the whole of England, and trace ancestral movements throughout the country at the touch of a button. Used in conjunction with the records of civil registration, the census enables us to trace the histories of families between 1841 and 1911.

Local historians can use the census for a wide variety of purposes. It provides much useful information for demographers, for the analysis of household and family structures, for the study of trades and occupations, and for mapping the pattern of migration. Entries for a particular household show, not just family members, but also the presence of servants, employees, and lodgers, providing valuable information for the social and economic historian. Much topographical information is also provided; this can be combined with the evidence of tithe maps and apportionments to recreate the physical structure of the village in the mid-nineteenth century. It can also be compared with the evidence of the Valuation Office survey to recreate that same structure as it was half a century later.

The census is perhaps the most important single source for local historians interested in the nineteenth century. It is easy to link it with other historical sources, such as the civil registers, rate books, trade directories, parish registers, electoral registers and poll books, and a variety of other records from parish chests, diocesan archives, Quarter Sessions and The National Archives (TNA). Such linkages can be useful to both family and local historians. Used with the census, they can help us reconstruct historical communities, and fill in the details of our ancestors' lives.

A census has been taken in England and Wales every ten years since 1801, except in 1941, when war intervened. Detailed statistics compiled from them have been published in the *Parliamentary papers* series, which are widely available in libraries. The returns themselves are in TNA, although they do not all survive. Census arrangements for Ireland and Scotland were different (see below, p. 43-6).

TNA does not hold manuscript returns for 1801, 1811, 1821, and 1831. Although nominal lists were sometimes compiled, they were not returned to London. They may occasionally be found in local record offices. For details, see below, p. 15. A few returns for later years have been damaged or lost. These are noted in the place-name indexes discussed below, p. 38.

TNA's holdings of post-1911 census returns are closed to the public for 100 years. Returns for 1931 were destroyed during World War II. For an interesting account of their destruction, see:

- 1931 Census
  yourarchives.nationalarchives.gov.uk/index.php?title=1931_Census

Census returns cannot be consulted directly. They would soon disintegrate if subjected to the amount of handling that they would receive. Instead, digitised images are available on the internet and CD. Microfilm and microfiche versions are also available, and are cheaper to consult, although most people will find that digitised images are much easier to use.

There are a number of works solely devoted to the census. The most comprehensive is:

- HIGGS, EDWARD. *Making sense of the census revisited: census records for England and Wales, 1801-1901.* Institute of Historical Research / National Archives, 2005.

For the history of the census, see:

- HIGGS, EDWARD. *Life, death and statistics: civil registration, censuses, and the work of the General Register Office, 1836-1952.* Local Population Studies, 2004.

Local historians will also find it useful to consult:

- LAWTON, RICHARD, ed. *The census and social structure: an interpretative guide to 19th century censuses for England and Wales.* Frank Cass, 1978.

Many studies on the census have been published in journals such as *Local population studies* and elsewhere. A comprehensive listing of articles and books published prior to 1989 is provided by:

- MILLS, DENNIS, & PEARCE, CAROL. *People and places in the Victorian census: a review and bibliography of publications based substantially on the manuscript census enumerators' books, 1841-1911.* Historical geography research series **23**. Historical Geography Research Group, 1989.

More recent studies can be identified in Higgs, or by searching:

- Royal Historical Society Bibliography
  www.rhs.ac.uk

A number of basic guides for family historians have been written. Most of the information they provide can be found in the present work. Some useful information is still provided by:

- LUMAS, SUSAN. *Making use of the census.* 4th ed. Public Record Office readers guide **1**. 2002.

The census is, of course, described in all family and local history handbooks. Particularly useful accounts are given in:

- HERBER, MARK. *Ancestral trails: the complete guide to British genealogy and family history.* 2nd ed. Sutton Publishing / Society of Genealogists, 2004.
- BEVAN, AMANDA. *Tracing your ancestor in The National Archives.* 7th ed. National Archives, 2006.
- MILLS, DENNIS, & DRAKE, MICHAEL. 'The census 1801-1991', in DRAKE, MICHAEL, & FINNEGAN, RUTH, eds. *Sources and methods for family and community historians: a handbook.* 2nd ed. Cambridge University Press,1997, p.25-56.

Recent works tend to emphasise the role of the Family Records Centre, which has now ceased operation (and is therefore ignored here). Most of the works mentioned above were published before they could take into account the astonishing developments in digitised databases which have occurred recently. These developments have rendered the census far easier to consult, and have opened it up to much greater investigation.

Digitisation has also introduced the term 'digitised image'. It is most important that researchers understand the difference between a digitised image and a transcript, and to avoid confusing these with the word 'index'. These terms are frequently used incorrectly. A census index is an alphabetical list of entries in the census, showing where to find them in either the original return, or in a transcript. A transcript should be an exact copy of the original census enumerator's book (although it rarely is). It is not in alphabetical order. Both are based on the original returns, or perhaps on digitised images. Digitised images are photographic copies of the original returns reproduced on computer screens, and therefore normally provide conclusive proof of the content of the originals. That does not necessarily apply to transcripts, much less to indexes.

The processes of transcribing and indexing leave plenty of room for error. An accuracy rate of over 95% is good. You therefore need access to the original returns, in order to check the information which has been copied. These, as already noted, cannot be produced for consultation. Hitherto, family historians have had to rely on microfiche or microfilm copies. Now, however, the returns for 1841 to 1911 have nearly all been digitised.

Digitised images (and microfilm) can generally be relied upon, unless the camera has accidentally missed a page, or cut one off in the middle. It may be easier to check an index or a transcript, but to be absolutely sure that the evidence provided by the census is accurate, you need to check digitised images, or microfilm.

Dates

Census dates are important. The census has normally recorded the names of people who were resident in a particular place on a particular night. It was taken on a Sunday, since that was the night when most people would be at home. The 1851 census was held two months earlier than its predecessors, because it was thought that fewer people would be absent from home at Easter than in the summer. Many people left home to get in the harvest during the summer months, sleeping in barns and outhouses, where it would be more difficult to count them. The census could not be taken earlier in the year, as the enumerators needed daylight to carry out their rounds. The dates of the census were as follows:

1801	10th March	1861	7th April
1811	27th May	1871	2nd April
1821	28th May	1881	3rd April
1831	29th May	1891	5th April
1841	6th June	1901	31st March
1851	30th March	1911	2nd April

Areas

The parish, the hundred (or its equivalent), and the county, were the units used by the earliest censuses. In 1841, they were replaced by the newly created registration districts and sub-districts, which were sub-divided to create enumeration districts (frequently parishes). When the returns reached the Census Office, however, they were re-arranged into the historical counties, sub-divided into hundreds, wapentakes, sokes, or liberties, and sub-divided again into parishes. This was done so that the statistics could be compared with those from earlier censuses.

From 1851, statistics were reported by registration districts, sub-districts, and enumeration districts. This means that there is a direct link between the census and the civil registers. If you know the registration district in which a marriage took place, you can search that district's census returns for information about the family. Conversely, the information in the census will help you search the civil registers.

Registration districts for particular places can be identified by consulting:
• Index of Places in England and Wales
  www.genuki.org.uk/big/eng/civreg/places
A full list of registration districts is provided by Lumas[1], and by:
• Registration Districts in England and Wales (1837-1974)
  www.ukbmd.org.uk/genuki/reg

Each registrar's sub-district was divided into a number of enumeration districts. These were originally intended to include c.200 houses. Registrars were responsible for sub-dividing or amalgamating them if there were substantial changes in population. However, emphasis was placed on retaining existing boundaries, in order to facilitate comparison between censuses. In 1901, over 3000 districts contained more than 1500 people, despite specific instructions that no district should have a population higher than this.

---

[1] LUMAS, SUSAN. *Making use of the census.* 4th ed. 2002, p.84-106.

Procedure

Parish overseers and incumbents were responsible for the administration of the first four censuses. In 1801, six questions were asked. Overseers had to answer three, the incumbent the other three. Answers had to be made on prescribed forms. Only statistics were required, not lists of names. However, some overseers did compile lists of names in order to count the numbers. Indeed, a number of printers unofficially printed forms to make the process easier. These sometimes survive amongst parish records (see below, p. 15). The official returns had to be attested before a JP, and handed to the High Constable for transmission to the Clerk of the Peace, and so to the Home Office.

In 1841, each new enumeration district became the responsibility of one enumerator. He or she was provided with detailed instructions, and delivered a schedule to each household in the district a few days before census night. These had to be filled in by household heads, who were also given detailed instructions. [Fig. 1] The schedules were collected by the enumerator after census night. In Wales, the household schedules were available in Welsh, although all enumerators' books were in English. Perhaps 50% of the population were illiterate in the early days of the census. If a householder or other informant was illiterate, then he or she might have to obtain assistance from some other person, or from the enumerator. In 1871, enumerators noted how many household schedules they completed for householders.

The illiteracy of householders could easily result in errors in the household schedules. Errors also resulted from the fact that enumerators asked questions that some people did not understand, or did not have sufficient information to answer. Sometimes, indeed, people answered questions that were not asked.

There were separate arrangements for large institutions such as hospitals, workhouses, and prisons. Their senior staff had to complete the schedules (see below, p. 24-5).

CENSUS OF THE POPULATION.

No. _____

1851.

HOUSEHOLDER'S SCHEDULE.

(Prepared under the direction of one of Her Majesty's Principal Secretaries of State.)

Parish or Township	
Town, Tything, Village, or Hamlet	
Street, Square, &c., or Road	
Name or No. of House	

To the Householder.

You are requested to insert the particulars specified on the other page, respecting all the persons who slept or abode in your house on the night of March 30th, in compliance with an Act which passed the House of Commons, and the House of Lords, in the last Session of Parliament, and received the assent of Her Majesty, the Queen, on the 5th of August, 1850.

This Paper will be called for on Monday, March 31st, by the appointed Officer,

and it will save trouble if, as the Act requires, you have the answers written in the proper columns by that time. It is his duty to verify the facts, and if you have omitted to comply with the above Instructions, to record them at your residence on that day.

Persons who refuse to give correct Information, incur a Penalty of Five Pounds; besides the inconvenience and annoyance of appearing, before two Justices of the Peace, and being convicted of having made a wilful mis-statement of age, or of any of the other particulars.

The Return is required to enable the Secretary of State to complete the Census, which is to show the number of the population—their arrangement by ages and families in different ranks, professions, trades, and employments—their distinction over the country in villages, towns, and cities—their increase and progress in the last ten years.

Approved,
G. GREY.

GEORGE GRAHAM,
Registrar General.

GENERAL INSTRUCTION.

This Schedule is to be filled up by the OCCUPIER or Person in charge of the house; if the house is let or sublet to different persons or families, in separate stories or apartments, the OCCUPIER or Person in charge of each such story or apartment must make a separate return, for his portion of the house upon a separate Householder's Schedule.

INSTRUCTIONS for filling up the Column headed "RANK, PROFESSION, or OCCUPATION."

The Superior Titles of PEERS and other Persons of RANK are to be inserted, as well as any high office which they may hold. Magistrates, Aldermen, and other important public officers to state their profession after their official title.

ARMY, NAVY, AND CIVIL SERVICE.—Add after the rank, "Artillery," "Royal Navy," &c. Persons in the CIVIL SERVICE to state the Department to which they are attached, after their title or rank; those on the Superannuation List to be so distinguished.

CLERGYMEN of the Church of England to return themselves as "Rector of ——," "Vicar of ——," "Curate of ——," &c., or as not having cure of souls. Protestant Ministers and Roman Catholic Priests to return themselves as such, and to state the name of the church or chapel in which they officiate. Dissenting Ministers to return themselves as "Independent Minister of ——," &c. Local or occasional preachers must return their ordinary occupations.

LEGAL PROFESSION.—Barristers to state whether or not in actual practice; Officers of any Court, &c., to state the description of office and name of Court. Solicitors' officers should distinguish whether "Solicitor," &c.

Members of the MEDICAL PROFESSION to state the University, College, or Hall, of which they are Graduates, Fellows, or Licentiates—also whether they practise as Physician, Surgeon, or General Practitioner, or are "not practising."

PROFESSORS, TEACHERS, PUBLIC WRITERS, Authors, and Scientific Men—to state the number of Science or Literature which they cultivate. Artist, the art which they cultivate. Graduates should enter their degrees in this column.

PERSONS ENGAGED IN COMMERCE, as Merchants, Brokers, Agents, &c.—to state the particular kind of business in which they are engaged, or the staple in which they deal.

The term FARMER to be applied only to the occupier of land, who is to be returned—"Farmer of [ ] acres, employing [12] labourers;" the number of acres, and of in and out-door labourers, on March 31st, being in all cases inserted. Sons or daughters employed at home or on the farm, may be returned—"Farmer's Son," "Farmer's Daughter."

In TRADES the Master is to be distinguished from the Journeyman and Apprentice, thus—Carpenter—Master employing [6] men / Apprentice; always the Carpenter of persons of the trade in his employ on March 31st.

In the case of WORKERS IN MINES OR MANUFACTURES, and generally in the co-operative ARTS, the particular branch of work, and the material, are always to be distinctly expressed if they are not implied in the name, as in Coal-miner, Brass-founder, Wool-carder, Silk-weaver, &c. Where the trade is much sub-divided, both sides and hands are to be returned thus—"Watchmaker—Finisher," "Printer—Compositor."

A person following the following trades own distinct trade may use the occupation in the code of their own importance.

MESSENGERS, PORTERS, LABOURERS, and SERVANTS, to be distinctly described according to the place and nature of their employment.

Persons following no Profession, Trade, or calling, and holding no public office, but deriving their incomes chiefly from land, houses, mines, or other real property, from dividends, interest of money, annuities, &c., may designate themselves "Landed Proprietor," "Proprietor of Houses," "Proprietor of Iron Mines," "Landed Proprietor," "Fund-holder," "Annuitant," &c., as the case may be. Person of advanced age who have retired from business to be entered thus—"Retired Silk Merchant," "Retired Watchmaker," &c.

ALMSPEOPLE, and persons in the receipt of parish relief should, after being described as such, have their previous occupations inserted.

WOMEN AND CHILDREN.—The titles or occupations of ladies who are householders to be entered according to the above instructions. The occupations of women who are regularly employed from home, or at home, in any but domestic duties, to be distinctly recorded. So also of children and young persons. Against the names of children above five years of age, if daily attending school, or receiving regular tuition under a master or governess at home, write "Scholar," and in the latter case add "at home."

EXAMPLES OF THE MODE OF FILLING UP THE RETURN.

Name and Surname.	Relation to Head of Family.	Condition.	Sex.	Age last Birth-day.	Rank, Profession, or Occupation.	Where Born.	If Deaf-and-Dumb or Blind.
George Wood	Head of Family	Married	M.	45	Farmer (of 111 acres employing 4 labourers)	Kent, Dartford	
Maria Wood	Wife	Married	F.	44	Farmer's Wife	Middlesex, Chelsea	
Emily Wood	Daughter	Unmarried	F.	22	Farmer's Daughter	Kent, Chislehurst	
Alan Wood	Son	Unmarried	M.	20	Farmer's Son	Kent, Chislehurst	
Florence Wood	Daughter		F.	14	Scholar	Kent, Beckenham	
Jane Holmes	Visitor	Widow	F.	39	Annuitant	Canada	
Eliza Edwards	Servant	Unmarried	F.	24	House Servant	Surrey, Greenwich	
Thomas Young	Servant	Unmarried	M.	18	Farm Labourer	Surrey, Croydon	
Janet Cox	Head of Family	Widow	F.	41	Glover	Scotland	
Sophia Cox	Daughter	Unmarried	F.	20	Dressmaker	Middlesex, Poplar	
Alexander Cox	Son	Unmarried	M.	18	Hand Loom Weaver (Silk)	Middlesex, Shoreditch	
William Cox	Son		M.	14	Errand Boy	Surrey, Lambeth	
Margaret Cox	Mother-in-law	Widow	F.	72	Formerly Laundress	Middlesex, Bethnal Green	Blind.
John Butler	Nephew	Unmarried	M.	24	Printer—Pressman	France (British Subject).	

Figure 1. Householders Instructions, 1851.

The details from household schedules were copied by the enumerators' into their books. The accuracy of their work varied, and was not necessarily as good as it should have been. An examination of enumerators' handwriting, and their attention to detail, may enable some judgement to be made on the value of their work. Emendations made by census clerks in London may also give clues to the reliability of the data.

The questions asked vary in different censuses, as will be described below. Preliminary and final pages in the census enumerators' books also differed. These pages provide a variety of information and statistics. Enumeration districts are fully described — a simple task in rural areas, but sometimes quite complicated in cities. Enumerators sometimes added interesting comments. The enumerator of All Hallows, Barking, for example, wrote a diatribe protesting about his paltry remuneration[2]. There were instructions and examples for the enumerator to study. Forms were provided for him to tabulate statistical information. Returns had to be signed by the enumerator, the registrar, and the superintendant registrar. Higgs[3] provides detailed descriptions of the enumerators' books for each census. Copies of enumerators' instructions for all census years can be viewed at **www.histpop.org**.

In 1841, most enumerators' returns were written in pencil, which is not always easily read on microfilm, although it may be clearer on computer screens. If the handwriting is difficult, and it is not easy to make out names, it may be useful to compare them with local directories, the electoral register, or other local name lists of the period. These will indicate the names that you might expect to find.

The enumerators' instructions did not specify the order in which households were to be entered in the books. However, they are frequently written in the order in which the enumerator collected the household schedules. The books may enable his path to be followed on the map, thus providing useful topographical evidence. That evidence may compensate for the frequent imprecision of the addresses given. The exact location of houses mentioned in early censuses is not necessarily easy to determine. Many houses were not numbered in the mid-nineteenth century, although the practice was being introduced. The Registrar General was still exhorting local authorities to number their streets in 1881.

The end of the entry for each household in the 1841 returns is recorded by one slash. Each house is divided from the next by two slashes. In 1851, short lines and long lines were drawn across the page for the same purpose. Similar conventions were used in subsequent censuses.

---

[2] Ibid, p.7.
[3] HIGGS, EDWARD. *Making sense of the census revisited: census records for England and Wales, 1801-1901.* 2005, p.169-88 & 197-200.

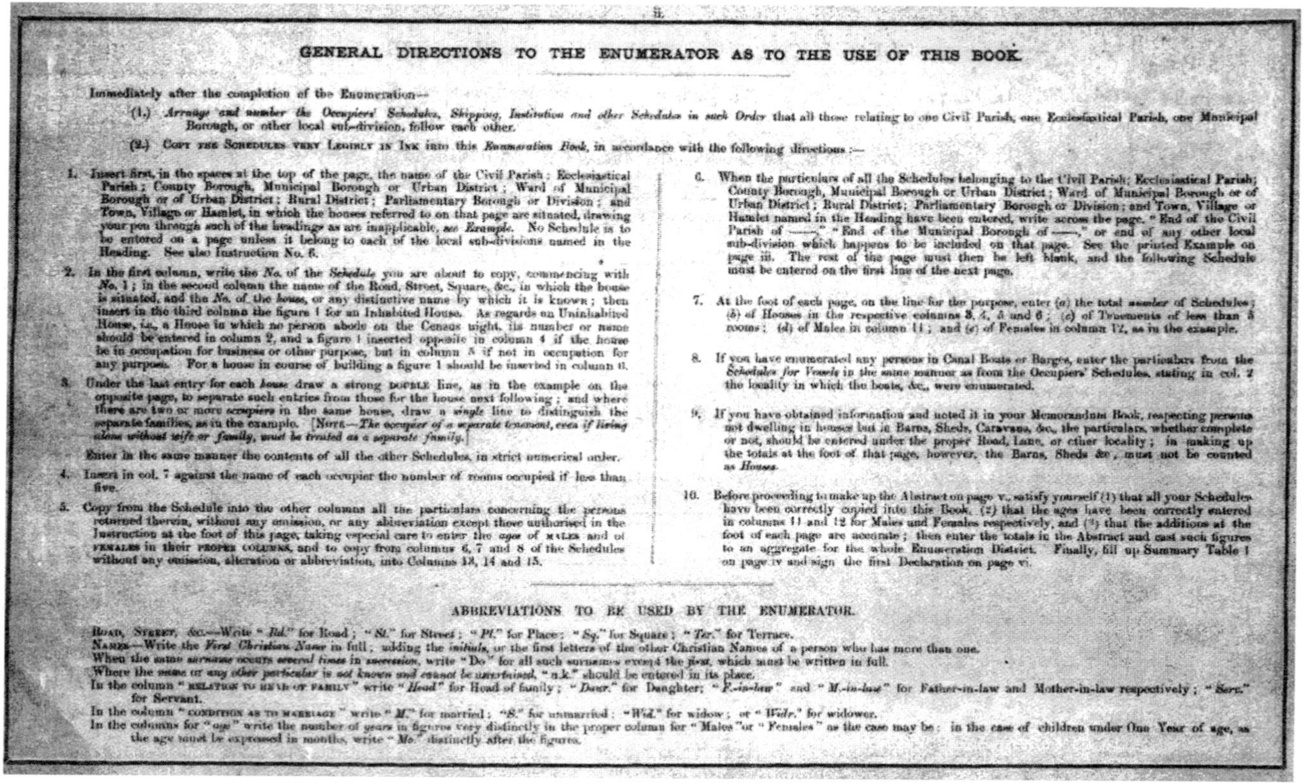

Figure 2. Enumerator's Instructions, 1901.

For the censuses of 1841 to 1901, both the census enumerators' books, and the household schedules, were sent to the Census Office. The books reveal much evidence of corrections made from the household schedules. The process of correction and extraction of statistics involved the correction and addition of information, the highlighting of information that had to be counted, and the ticking of information that had been counted. As a result, the many markings made by Census Office clerks sometimes make the books appear to be much the worse for wear, and may make them difficult to read. This effect is made worse by the fact that the images we see on computer screens, and particularly on microfilm readers, are generally in black and white. Much of the original work was done in colour, which cannot be seen.

Unfortunately, for 1901 and earlier censuses, the household schedules were destroyed after they had been checked. It is the census enumerators' books which survive. For 1911, however, the original household schedules were preserved, and are being made available as digitised images. Enumerators' summary books will also be available, although these do not give full particulars relating to individuals.

Statistics based upon the census enumerators' books were published in the *Parliamentary papers* series. These *reports* provide much useful information for local historians. They do not, however, record names, although they may provide interesting background information for family historians. The *Parliamentary papers* are widely available in libraries. A brief guide to the statistical *reports* is provided by:
- The Census, 1801-1901: Statistical Reports
  www.nationalarchives.gov.uk/catalogue/researchguidesindex.as
  Click title

For a more detailed guide, see:
- *Guide to census reports, Great Britain, 1801-1966.* H.M.S.O., 1977.

The reports themselves have been digitised, and can be read at:
- Histpop: the Online Historical Population Reports Website
  www.histpop.org
  This site also has many interesting essays on various aspects of the census.

See also:
- Victorian Census Project
  www.staffs.ac.uk/schools/humanities_and_soc_sciences/census/vichome.htm

The statistics themselves are now readily available at:
- A Vision of Britain through Time
  www.visionofbritain.org.uk

For a review of this site, see:
- SOUTHALL, H. 'A Vision of Britain through Time: making sense of 200 years of census reports', *Local population studies*, **76**, 2006, p.76-89.

The Censuses of 1801-1831

The earliest official censuses, ar already noted, were compiled by overseers and clergymen. They did not require the names of inhabitants to be recorded. The 1801 questions are shown in the box.

1801 Questions to Overseers

1. 'How many Inhabited Houses are there in your Parish, Township, or Place; by how many Families are they occupied; and, how many Houses therein are Uninhabited?'
2. 'How many persons (including Children of whatever Age) are there actually found within the Limits of your Parish, Township, or Place, at the Time of taking this Account, distinguishing Males and Females, and exclusive of Men actually serving in His Majesty's Regular Forces or Militia, and exclusive of Seamen either in His Majesty's Service, or belonging to Registered Vessels?'
3. 'What Number of Persons, in your Parish, Township, or Place, are chiefly employed in Agriculture; how many in Trade, Manufactures, or Handicraft; and, how many are not comprised in any of the preceding Classes?'

1801 Questions to Incumbents

4. 'What was the Number of Baptisms and Burials in your Parish, Township, or Place, in the several Years, 1700, 1710, 1720, 1730, 1740, 1750, 1760, 1770, 1780, and each subsequent Year to the 31st Day of December 1800, distinguishing Males from Females?'
5. 'What has been the Number of Marriages in your Parish, Township, or Place, in each Year, from the Year 1754 inclusive to the End of the Year 1800?'
6. 'Are there any Matters which you think it necessary to remark in Explanation of your Answers to any of the preceding Questions?'

In 1811, these questions were revised. Unoccupied houses were distinguished from new houses being built. The question on occupation related to families rather than to individuals. And the clergy were asked to record the number of baptisms, marriages and burials in each of the preceding ten years.

Further refinements followed in subsequent censuses. In 1821, there was an attempt to determine the age structure of the population. In 1831, much more detailed questions on occupations were asked, and the clergy had to count the number of illegitimate children born in 1830.

The returns sent to London for most of these censuses have been destroyed. Only the clergymen's returns of 1831 survive in TNA (HO 71). Most of the information provided in these is recorded in the published census reports.

Despite the destruction of the official returns, about 800 listings of inhabitants compiled for these censuses were retained by their compilers, and survive in local archives. A few of these give full household enumerations, but most simply record the names of the heads of households, their occupations, and the numbers of people in each household. Some provide information that was not requested by the official census. For example, the 1801 enumeration for Smalley, Derbyshire, includes notes on bastardy cases. These listings are particularly common in Yorkshire and East Anglia, where they are frequently compiled on forms which were unofficially printed. Gibson and Medlycott (below, p. 26) list these returns. A fuller listing is given in:

- WALL, RICHARD, WOOLLARD, MATTHEW, & MORING, BEATRICE. *Census schedules and listings 1801-1831: an introduction and guide.* Working paper series 5. University of Essex Dept. of History, 2004. This is also available online at **www.histpop.org.uk/pre41**

The Census of 1841
The returns for 1841 included columns headed:
- 'Place'
- 'Houses: uninhabited or building'
- 'Houses: inhabited'
- 'Names of each person who abode therein the preceding night'
- 'Age and Sex: Male'
- 'Age and Sex: Female'
- Profession, trade employment or of independent means
- Where born: whether born in same county
- Where born: whether born in Scotland, Ireland, or foreign parts

All of these columns require some comment. The lack of precision with which particular houses were identified in the 'place' column of early censuses has already been commented upon. Sometimes it is just the name of the hamlet, or even the parish, that is given.

The column for houses may sometimes provide useful topographical information. Empty houses are mentioned, and it may be possible to identify them. This could be useful to the local historian in areas such as Cornish mining districts, where population was in decline. There is space at the foot of the 'houses' column to total the number of houses recorded.

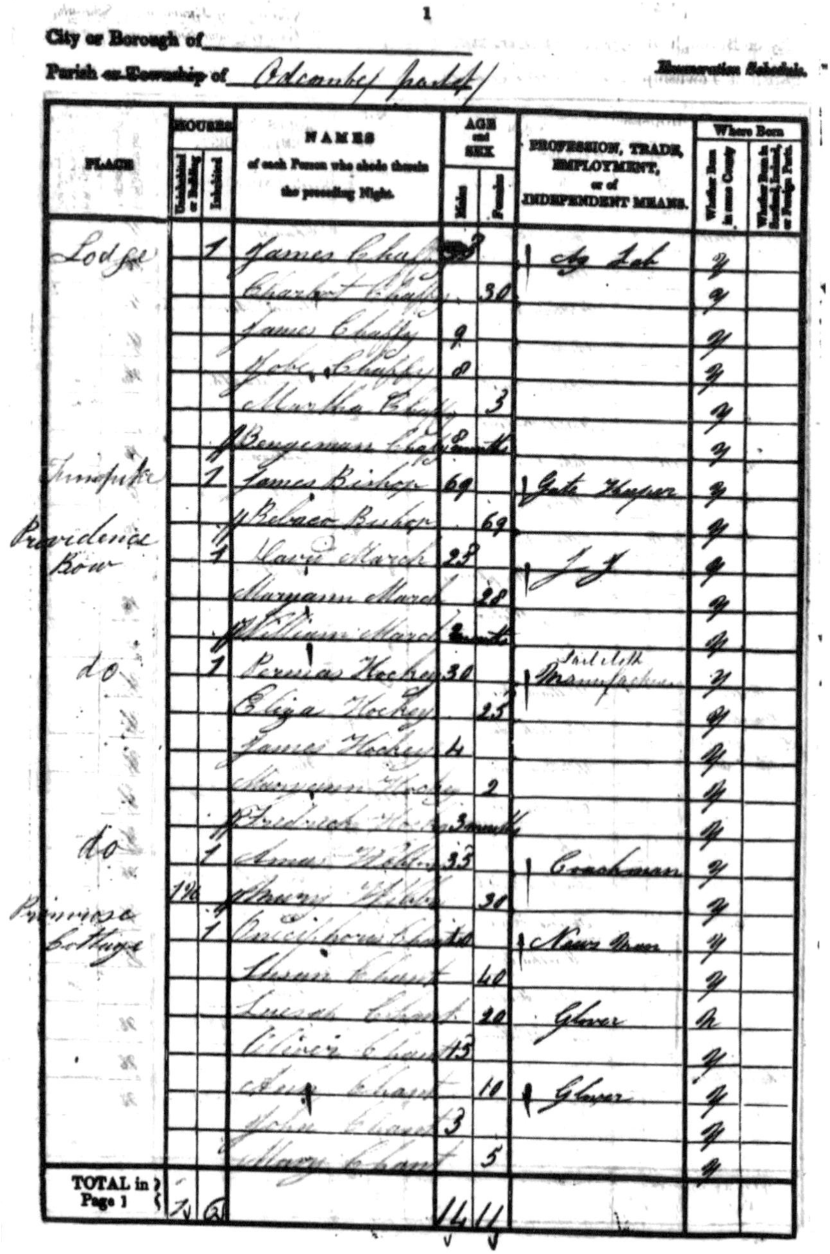

Figure 3. TNA HO 107/906/13, f.18. Census Return, 1841, for Odcombe. Note the entry for the Hockey family, who are discussed on p. 46-8.

Names of the residents in a particular house commence with the head of the household. Returns do not, however, indicate his or her relationship to the other residents. A man and a woman of the same age living together may be husband and wife, but they may also be brother and sister, or have some other relationship. It is unwise to infer relationships without other evidence, such as civil registration certificates. The absence of the head of a household sometimes confused enumerators: how to describe the only person in a house on census night if he or she was a servant to the (absent) head of the household?

Enumerators were instructed to record only one forename. If your ancestor had two or more, only one will be recorded.

The names recorded in the census were not necessarily the only people normally resident in the house. Individuals who happened to be absent on census night were not recorded at their home address. They were recorded at the place where they spent census night, whether that was in a hotel, a prison, on board ship, or wherever they found a bed (if they did!). If, however, they were on a night shift, they should have been recorded at their usual residence.

There is space at the foot of the age and sex columns to total the numbers of males and females recorded. The information regarding age is not precise. With the exception of children under 15, ages were usually rounded down to the nearest figure divisible by five. Hence someone aged 63 would have been recorded as aged 60. This is likely to explain minor discrepancies between the age as given in the census, and ages as recorded in other sources, such as subsequent censuses, or the civil registers.

Greater discrepancies in ages recorded may not be so easily explained. The information given to enumerators was not always correct. Householders, who were responsible for making the returns, did not necessarily know the exact ages of other residents. And if they did, they may have had reason to conceal them. The number of females aged 30 to 40 in most census years does not correlate with the number of females aged 20 to 30 in the immediately previous census years, even allowing for deaths. That can only be explained by female vanity! Others falsified their ages in order to claim the status of adults, which may have been important to them for keeping a job, or for getting married.

The 'occupations' column was perhaps the most subjective, as occupations reflected men's social as well as economic status. That gave an opportunity to inflate reputations by recording, for instance, 'horseman' rather than 'agricultural labourer'. In general, the occupations of men in full-time employment present few problems of interpretation. The recording of womens' work is much more problematic, as is the analysis of seasonal, casual and part-time work. Such work was frequently not recorded.

The 'where born' column is not much use for family historians. If a person was born in the county in which he is recorded, the answer to the question 'whether born in same county' will be yes (or perhaps 'Y'). That eliminates searching in other counties, but is not of much real help. If the answer is 'no', or 'N', then there is little indication of where to search next, unless the initials 'I', S', or 'F' are used for Ireland, Scotland, and 'foreign parts' respectively.

The Censuses of 1851 to 1901

Census returns from 1851 onwards are more detailed, and enable links to be made with other data sources much more easily. For example, details of relationships and birthplaces are given, enabling both civil and parish registers to be checked.

1851 returns are headed with geographical information. This includes the name of the 'parish or township', and gives space for details of the 'ecclesiastical district', 'city or borough', 'town', or 'village'. These categories were altered in subsequent census years, reflecting legislation which created new administrative areas. In 1881, for example, the headings were 'Civil Parish (or township) of ...', 'City or Municipal Borough of ...', 'Municipal Ward of ....', 'Parliamentary Borough of ...', 'Town or Village or Hamlet of ...', 'Urban Sanitary District of ...', 'Rural Sanitary District of ...', and 'Ecclesiastical District or Parish of ...'.

Columns of the 1851 returns are headed:
- 'No. of Householder's Schedule'
- 'Name of Street, Place or Road, and Name or No. of House'
- 'Name and Surname of each Person who abode in the house on the Night of the 30th March 1851'
- 'Relation to Head of Family'
- 'Condition'
- 'Age of Male'
- 'Age of Female'
- 'Rank, Profession or Occupation'
- 'Where born'
- 'Whether Blind, or Deaf and Dumb'

The enumerators' books, as already noted, were compiled from householders schedules. From 1851, houses were numbered in the returns. Numbering them enabled a better check to be kept on whether they were all transcribed correctly by the enumerator, and distinguishes between houses in the books. Local historians may find these numbers useful to ensure that the returns they are using are complete.

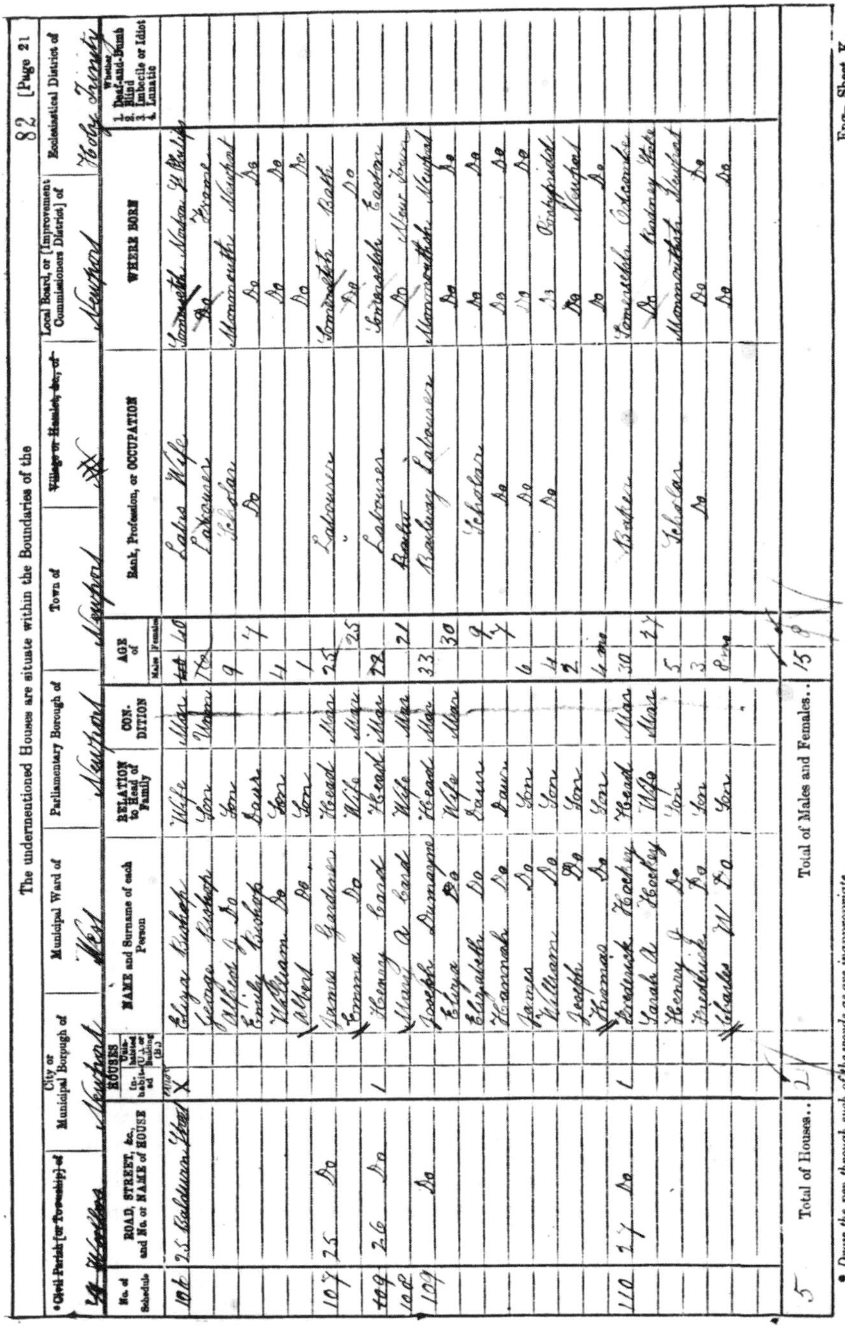

The undermentioned Houses are situate within the Boundaries of the — 82 [Page 21

*Civil Parish [or Township] of	City or Municipal Borough of	Municipal Ward of	Parliamentary Borough of	Town of	Village or Hamlet, &c., of	Local Board, or [Improvement Commissioners District] of	Ecclesiastical District of
St Woollos	Newport	West	Newport	Newport	X	Newport	Holy Trinity

No. of Schedule	ROAD, STREET, &c., and No. or NAME of HOUSE	HOUSES Inhabited	HOUSES Uninhabited (U.) or Building (B.)	NAME and Surname of each Person	RELATION to Head of Family	CONDITION	AGE of Males	AGE of Females	Rank, Profession, or OCCUPATION	WHERE BORN	Whether 1. Deaf-and-Dumb 2. Blind 3. Imbecile or Idiot 4. Lunatic
106	25 Baldwin Street	X		Eliza Bishop	Wife	Mar		40	Labrs Wife	Somersetsh Norton St Philips	
				George Bishop	Son	Unm	18		Labourer	Do Frome	
				Alfred J Do	Son		9		Scholar	Monmouth Newport	
				Emily Bishop	Daur			7	Do	Do Do	
				William Do	Son		4			Do Do	
				Albert Do	Son		1			Do Do	
107	25 Do			James Gardiner	Head	Mar	25		Labourer	Somersetsh Bath	
				Emma Do	Wife	Mar		25		Do Do	
108	26 Do	1		Henry Card	Head	Mar	22		Labourer	Somersetsh Easton	
				Mary A Card	Wife	Mar		21	Baker	Do New Town	
109	Do			Joseph Dumayne	Head	Mar	33		Railway Labourer	Monmouthsh Newport	
				Eliza Do	Wife	Mar		30		Do Do	
				Elizabeth Do	Daur			9	Scholar	Do Do	
				Hannah Do	Daur			7	Do	Do Do	
				James Do	Son		6		Do	Do Do	
				William Do	Son		4		Do	Do Pontypridd	
				Joseph Do	Son		2			Do Newport	
				Thomas Do	Son		4 mo			Do Do	
110	27 Do	1		Frederick Hockey	Head	Mar	30		Baker	Somersetsh Odcombe	
				Sarah A Hockey	Wife	Mar		27		Do Rodney Stoke	
				Henry J Do	Son		5		Scholar	Monmouthsh Newport	
				Frederick Do	Son		3		Do	Do Do	
				Charles W Do	Son		8 mo			Do Do	
5	Total of Houses..	2			Total of Males and Females..		15	8			

* Draw the pen through such of the words as are inappropriate.

Eng– Sheet K.

Figure 4. TNA RG 10/4346, f.82. Census return, 1871, for Newport. See p. 46-8. for a discussion of the Hockey family entry.

Household Record

Search results | Download

Previous Household   Next Household

Household:

Name	Relation	Marital Status	Gender	Age	Birthplace	Occupation	Disability
Frederick HOKEY	Head	M	Male	40	Somerset, England	Master Baker Employ 1 Man 2 Boys	
Sarah Ann HOKEY	Wife	M	Female	37	Somerset, England		
Henry John HOKEY	Son	U	Male	15	Newport, Monmouth, England	Bakers Asst	
Frederick HOKEY	Son	U	Male	13	Newport, Monmouth, England		
Charles W. HOKEY	Son	U	Male	10	Newport, Monmouth, England		
Clementina E. J. HOKEY	Daur	U	Female	8	Newport, Monmouth, England		
Ada HOKEY	Daur	U	Female	6	Newport, Monmouth, England		
Samuel HOKEY	Son	U	Male	3	Newport, Monmouth, England		
Mabel E. HOKEY	Daur	U	Female	5 m	Newport, Monmouth, England		
Mary MARSH	Serv	U	Female	19	Newport, Monmouth, England		

Source Information:

Dwelling	27 Baldwin St
Census Place	St Woollos, Monmouth, Wales
Family History Library Film	1342266
Public Records Office Reference	RG11
Piece / Folio	5264 / 40
Page Number	14

Figure 5. Transcript of the 1881 census return from the Family Search website **www.familysearch.org**. See p. 46-8 for a discussion of the Hockey family entry.

Used by permission 1999-2002 Intellectual Reserve Inc. All rights reserved.

Places were better recorded than in 1841, although it was not until the 1880s that most streets had their houses numbered. Even then, the numbering was sometimes done in odd sequences, and it was not unknown for an entire street to be re-numbered, making comparison with previous censuses difficult. If a particular household lived at no. 10 in the 1881 census, and in the same street, but at a different number, in 1891, it does not necessarily mean that the household moved. They may have simply been re-numbered.

It is also not unknown for a street to be in two separate enumeration districts. Even more confusing is the fact that many street names have changed, especially in London. In some cases, whole areas were demolished and rebuilt to a different layout. Many streets which existed in 1841 are now under railway terminals or blocks of high rise flats. See below, p.38, for details of how to find particular streets in the census.

The recording of names also slightly changed. In 1851, there were no instructions regarding the inclusion of second forenames. For 1861 to 1901, initials were to be given.

1851 and subsequent returns do include one vital addition to the information previously required. They record the relationship of each inhabitant to the head of the household. They therefore provide almost incontrovertible identification of wives and children. This identification is made even more definite by the column for 'condition', that is, whether married, unmarried, widow, or widower. Be careful, however. The terms used in the nineteenth century are not necessarily used in the same way today. 'Son-in-law', for example, may mean step-son rather than daughter's husband. 'Brother' may mean brother-in-law. 'Son' may mean grandson. Even the term 'wife' may be misleading; enumerators sometimes made the mistake of writing 'wife' when they meant 'son's wife', i.e. daughter-in-law.

From 1851, ages given were not rounded down, as they had been in 1841. In 1881, the question posed was 'age at last birthday'. Studies have demonstrated that, in a substantial percentage of cases, ages reported in one census are inconsistent with the ages reported in the succeeding census. Few, however, are out by more than two years.

Punch's 1861 Comments on the Fair Sex and the Census
'Pray, Ladies, have you made your minds up as to what age you intend to be for the next ten years? Because the seventh of April, dears, is drawing sadly nigh at hand, and you had better be prepared to answer this momentous question. It would be awkward to be taken by surprise at the last moment, and to let the truth slip out in the presence of a maid-servant, from whom you have for months, perhaps, been carefully concealing it. Of course we should not dream of charging you with planning how to shirk the fact, and send in false returns, any more than we could think you'd wear false ringlets in your hair, or grow false roses on your cheeks. But accidents will happen in the best regulated households, and avoid them as one may there will always be mistakes. Moreover, some ladies are apt, by the mere weakness of their sex, to let their inclinations get the better of their actions, so that their heads are often guided by their hearts, instead of being biased by the judgment of their heads. Thus it happens when a census sheet is set before her, Lovely Woman makes (unconsciously of course) a wrong return, and states what she would wish to be instead of

what she is. We have known ladies in this way so completely lose their natural control over their limbs, as to let themselves record the somewhat startling information that they are several years younger than they were ten years ago, while many a 'little sister' who, when the census was last taken was reported as eighteen, has only reached in the past decade the ripe age of twenty-one. Nay, in a case which we can vouch for as having come under our notice, a lady called herself but two years only older than her daughter, and such was her bewilderment at being asked her age she could not be persuaded she had made any mistake.

Entries in the occupations column continued to be subjective, although householders and enumerators were given more detailed instructions on how they should be recorded (see fig. 2). From 1851, children were frequently described as 'scholars'. Such entries may be used to trace educational provision. They may also hide the fact that children were working, perhaps illegally.

The 'where born' column is particularly valuable for family historians, although precise information is not always given. Usually a parish, town or city is mentioned, although sometimes it may be just a county, or, if born overseas, the country. This column may help to identify entries in civil and parish registers. That depends, of course, on whether the information is accurate, and on how precise it is.

The householder had to provide the information. But he did not necessarily have it. He may not have known, for example, where his servant was born. His spelling of placenames may easily lead to confusion, and his grasp of geography may not have been great. It is not uncommon for places to be misplaced, for example, Birmingham in Staffordshire, or Kendal in Lancashire.

Deliberate falsification may also have occurred. Birthplace was an important category for the poor, who were liable to be removed to their place of settlement, and who may therefore have given false information.

Birthplace information must not be mis-interpreted. It does not record all movements between the date of birth and the date of the census. It shows the net result of perhaps many moves, as at the date of the census.

After 1851, there were a number of minor adjustments to the information requested by the census enumerator. From 1871, the categories of 'imbecile' and 'idiot' were added to the column requesting information about the blind, deaf and dumb. In 1891, this became 'lunatic, imbecile, or idiot'. The precise difference between these terms is unclear. It is, however, clear that the information elicited was hopelessly inaccurate, largely due to the pejorative connotations of the word 'idiot'. This was revealed by a check done immediately after the 1881 census. The names of 'idiots' admitted to a large asylum in the twelve months immediately following were checked against the relevant entries in the 1881 returns. Only half of the cohort aged 5-15 were described by enumerators as 'idiots'. When the term 'feeble-minded' was substituted for 'idiot' in 1901, numbers recorded rose markedly. People did not like to admit that they had an 'idiot' in the family.

This question sometimes elicited information that had not actually been requested. Infirmities other than those specified were sometimes identified. A 'rheumatic cripple' was mentioned in a return from North Cardiganshire, and the mate of the Guiseppe Guippa, docked in Cardiff Harbour in 1871, was a eunuch.[4]

Further questions were added in 1891. Enumerators were asked to record the number of rooms (if less than 5) occupied by a family, and to indicate whether workers were employers, employees, or neither of these. The latter category appears to have been used for the self-employed who had no employees. In 1901, this was changed to 'Employer, Worker, or Own Account'.

Questions about language also found a place in 1891 and 1901. In Wales, these censuses note whether Welsh was spoken. The language of children under 3 was not, however, recorded.

For detailed discussions of the 1891 and 1901 censuses, from the local historian's point of view, see:

* SCHURER, K. 'The 1891 census and local population studies', *Local population studies* 47, 1991, p.16-29.
* WOOLLARD, MATTHEW. 'The 1901 census: an introduction', *Local population studies* 67, 2001, p.26-43.

The Census of 1911

The returns for 1911 are currently being released.

The documents to be made available differ from those of previous censuses. The householders' schedules have been preserved, as have enumerators' summary books. Details of individuals will be found in the householders' schedules. The enumerators' summary books provide information on buildings and housing, but only note the names of 'occupiers', that is, householders. Examples of both householders' schedules and enumerators' summary books can be viewed at **www.histpop.org**.

A number of new questions were asked in 1911. Family historians will find the additional information provided for married women invaluable. Householders were required to state the number of years married, and

---

[4] Higgs, op cit, p.94.

the number of children born to the marriage, whether living or deceased. There is also more information on the industries in which people worked, which will be useful to local historians. More details of the 1911 census can be found at:
- 1911 Census
  www.1911census.org.uk

Special Returns : Institutions, Soldiers, Seamen, etc.
Household schedules were the norm in the census. However, not everyone was resident in a normal household. Many were in hospitals, workhouses, prisons, and other institutions. The crews of ships had to be counted, as did soldiers in barracks.

Large institutions were treated as enumeration districts in their own right. The definition of 'large' varied in 1841, but in 1851 it was supposed to include every institution with over 200 inmates. This was reduced to 100 in 1891. Institutions which fell below this number were treated as ordinary households.

Special forms were devised for institutional returns. These did not record the home addresses of inmates, but only the address of the institution. There was a column for 'position in the institution' in 1851, and for 'relation to head of family or position in the institution' thereafter. Preliminary tables total the number of officers, members of officers families, and inmates. They also note the number of males and females per page.

For the family historian, returns from institutions are less valuable than ordinary returns. Unless several family members were present in the same institution, they do not show family relationships. The officers responsble for making the returns were less likely than heads of households to have accurate details of ages, places of birth, and occupations. They frequently attempted to make informed guesses, or wrote 'NK' - not known. It may be impossible even to identify inmates, since sometimes only initials were given in the name column. In 1861, the relevant column was headed 'name and surname or initials of inmates', providing authorisation for this practice.

Soldiers in UK barracks were enumerated in the same way. Less information was gathered for those serving overseas. Until 1911, the military authorities were asked to provide statistics of officers, other ranks, wives, and children, either by regiment, or by place. No other enumeration took place.

The Royal Navy received more detailed attention. Those who served in shore establishments were recorded in either household or institutional returns. In 1841, those at sea on census night were counted in the same way as soldiers overseas. In 1851 special enumeration books were issued to commanding officers, but these have been lost. Those for subsequent censuses have survived. For 1861 to 1881, these had columns for name and surname, rank or rating (quality in 1861), condition, age, and birthplace. Passengers had to be listed as well as seamen. For 1891 and 1901, there were columns for name and surname, relation to vessel (i.e. crew or passenger), condition as to marriage, age last birthday, profession or occupation, whether employer, employee, or self-employed (for passenges only), birthplace, and medical disabilities.

The arrangements for counting merchant seamen were very complex, and cannot be described here in detail. A fuller description is given by Higgs[5]. Enumeration was spread over a period of time, rather than being taken on a single census day. In 1841, there was no enumeration on board ships. Instead, a global figure was calculated from the registers held by the Registrar of Shipping and Seamen. In 1851, a full enumeration on board ships in ports and in home waters was taken. The Registrar attempted a head count for ships outside of home waters. Unfortunately, few returns survive from this census. However, similar arrangements were made for subsequent censuses. Ships' schedules can found with the census enumerators books.

Abbreviations Used by Enumerators
A variety of abbreviations were used by census enumerators. The following list includes some that were common.

Ag Lab	Agricultural Labourer
Ap	Apprentice
BS	British subject
Cl	Clerk
do	Ditto
F	Foreign parts
FS	Female servant
FWK	Framework Knitter
HP	Half pay (officer of the armed forces not working, but retained on half pay)
I	Ireland
Ind	Independent - living on own capital
J	Journeyman (qualified tradesman working for wages)
M	Manufacturer
Mar	Married
Mo	Month(s)
MS	Male Servant
NK	Not known
P	Armed forces pensioner
Rail Lab	Railway labourer

---

[5] Higgs, op cit, p.48-52.

S	Scotland
Serv	Servant
Sh	Shopman
Unm	Unmarried
Wid	Widow/Widower

Other Population Censuses

In addition to the official returns of 1841 to 1901, there are a wide range of other population enumerations giving the names of inhabitants. The unofficial returns to the censuses of 1801-1831 have already been discussed. Other censuses were taken for a wide range of reasons. Clergy were responsible for many; they compiled, for example, Easter books listing communicants, and incumbents' visitors books. Larger surveys include the Compton census of 1676[6], which assessed the extent of non-conformity nation-wide. 19 parish listings of inhabitants survive. There are also extensive listings from the Archdeaconry of Stafford, 1532/3[7], and the Diocese of St. Asaph in the 1680s.[8]

Poor law overseers and guardians sometimes listed local inhabitants, as did parish and borough authorities. Such listings could be useful in making rate assessments, or determining the distribution of poor relief. A variety of other institutions and people also found reasons to conduct local censuses. A full survey of local listings is provided by:

- GIBSON, JEREMY, & MEDLYCOTT, MERVYN. *Local census listings, 1522-1930: holdings in the British Isles.* 3rd ed. FFHS, 1997 (2001 reprint).

See also:

- CHAPMAN, COLIN. *Pre-1841 censuses and population listings.* 2nd ed. Lochin Publishing, 1991.

A wide range of other name lists, such as tax lists, electoral registers, pollbooks, militia lists, loyalty oath rolls, *etc.*, are also available. These can be used as census substitutes, but are beyond the scope of this book. A separate booklet dealing with them in the present series is planned.

Associated Censuses

Governments have taken advantage of the decennial population census to make enquiries on a variety of other matters at the same time. An agricultural census was taken in 1801. Acreage returns in TNA (HO 67)

---

[6] WHITEMAN, ANNE, ed. *The Compton census of 1676: a critical edition.* Oxford University Press, 1986.

[7] KETTLE, ANN J., ed. *A list of families in the Archdeaconry of Stafford, 1532-3.* Collections for a history of Staffordshire 4th series **8**. Staffordshire Record Society, 1976.

[8] 'St. Asaph notitiae' **www.llgc.org.uk/Notitiae/nll_s001.htm.**

show the acreage devoted to different crops in each parish. This is fully transcribed in:

- *Home Office Acreage Returns (HO 67) Lists and Analysis.* List and Index Society **189, 190, 195 & 196**. 1982-3.

The 1851 census was accompanied by inquiries concerning both religion and education. A similar education census was taken again in 1871. The religious census lists all churches and places of worship, and records the number attending services on census Sunday. The clergy of the established church were horrified to discover that there were more nonconformists than Anglicans. See:

- Ecclesiastical Census of 1851
  www.nationalarchives.gov.uk/catalogue/
  RdLeaflet.asp?sLeafletID=126
- Bums on Pews: the Religious Census of 1851
  www.fachrs.com/pages/members/papers/b_o_p.htm
- THOMPSON, DAVID M. 'The religious census of 1851', in LAWTON, RICHARD, ed. *The census and social structure.* Frank Cass, 1978, p.241-86.

A few returns have been printed. See, for example:

- ROBINSON, DAVID, ed. *The 1851 religious census: Surrey.* Surrey Record Society **35**. 1997.

The original returns of the educational census have not survived. However, a printed report in the *Parliamentary papers* series gives enrolment and attendance figures for boys and girls at both day and Sunday schools. A similar census was taken in 1871. The 1851 census is fully described in:

- GOLDSTROM, J.M. 'Education in England and Wales in 1851: the education census of Great Britain, 1851', in LAWTON, RICHARD, ed. *The census and social structure.* Frank Cass, 1978, p.224-40.

Census Problems for Family & Local Historians

A variety of problems may arise when using the census enumerators' books. Some of these have already been mentioned. The data may be incorrect. Some respondents felt the need to alter their ages, to give false names, to inflate their social status, or to hide their places of birth from the poor law authorities. Census enumerators also made mistakes. So did transcribers and indexers. Spelling and handwriting are not always easy to understand.

The interpretation of the census may also be problematic. It is vital to understand how enumerators went about their business before using the raw data provided in enumerators' books or in census reports.

Incorrect data may be due to falsification, or simply to mistakes.

There were plenty of opportunities for mistakes to be made. Both house-holders and enumerators were capable of jumping to hasty and erroneous conclusions. Householders, and, more particularly, the people responsible for recording data in prisons, hotels, ships, and other institutions, did not necessarily know when or where people were born. They may have made guesses that were more or less informed. They may also have been illiterate, and obliged to ask others to write down the information that they had. It is also probable that some people did not know their own ages, or where they were born. The enumerators themselves made mistakes when copying information from householders' schedules into their own books. Many corrections were written on the returns by clerks at the Census Office.

Transcribers and indexers are also not perfect. They make mistakes. If an indexer mis-spells a name, or fails to enter it altogether, the chances of finding that name in the index are much diminished. If you cannot find a name that you know ought to be there, try using a different index, another database, or consult the original census on microfilm.

Spelling sometimes presents problems. It is normally assumed today that there is only one way to spell a name. For the nineteenth century, that is a false assumption. Spelling did vary. If you do not find an entry for Smith, try Smythe. Osborn might be Osbourn. Guilford might be Guildford. Always check as many variant spellings as you can.

Handwriting has already been mentioned as a possible problem, especially for 1841, when enumerators used pencils. Census returns frequently have a variety of ticks and other marks on them, which sometimes obscure writing. Some letters are particularly prone to mis-interpretation. For example, minims in letters such as w, m, n and u can easily be read incorrectly. An 'a' may look like an 'o'. 'I' was sometimes used for 'J', 'R' could sometimes look like 'P' or 'M', and 'L' and 'S' are sometimes difficult to distinguish. It can be easy to read 'sawyer' as 'lawyer' or vice versa. If in doubt, compare the entry you want to interpret with other entries where the same letters are used, and check how the enumerator writes them.

People may also be difficult to find because they have changed their name. There were many reasons for changing personal names. Our ancestors married and re-married, with the women changing their surnames on each occasion. Men also altered their surnames. Foreigners anglicised theirs. Bigamists sought to conceal their real names. Heirs were sometimes required to change their name in order to inherit.

You may also fail to find people because the enumerators failed to find them. The 1841 census was taken in June, when many itinerants were on the move, and were sleeping in barns, sheds, or perhaps in the open air. No special arrangements were made to count them, although enumerators were instructed to record their numbers in the preliminary pages of their books. In 1851, the census was put back to the end of March, in order to reduce the problem. Nevertheless, many itinerants must have escaped enumeration, and probably continue to do so to this day.

Another source of failure was the tendency for parents not to enter new-born babies who had not been baptised. This was a hang-over from the idea that such children were outside the Kingdom of God. As late as 1911, the number of children under two recorded in the census was 68% short of the number of births registered in the previous two years[9].

Understanding the census is not necessarily straightforward. There have been many studies of census methodology. Some are listed by Higgs[10], who himself provides extensive guidance. Reference may also be made to the bibliography by Mills & Pearce (above, p.6)

An essential preliminary for local historians is some knowledge of statistical methods and sampling techniques. These are not difficult to understand. A good introduction is provided by:

• FLOUD, RODERICK. *An introduction to quantitative methods for historians.* Routledge, 2005.

Researchers need to be aware of the way in which enumerators collected data, and to ask whether the instructions they had were followed properly. They also need to view the questions asked in the census critically, and to appreciate that questions were not always answered in the way the authorities anticipated. Changes in procedures, and in the questions asked in successive censuses, need to be understood before comparisons can be made over time. So do changes in the boundaries of enumeration districts. The official *census reports* (see above, p. 13) need to be read in order to understand the background to the raw statistics. They provide excellent guides to the difficulties involved in interpreting the data.

Study of these reports will reveal how the census office defined terms such as 'household', 'unoccupied house', and 'room'. These terms might appear to have obvious meanings, but the appearance can be deceptive. For example, were lodgers members of someone else's household, or were they householders in their own right?[11] Was a house being built an 'unoccupied house'? Was a landing a 'room'? Such questions caused difficulty to householders and enumerators, as well as to the modern researcher.

Occupational terms are also problematic, especially in view of the fact that they often denoted status as well as occupation. Indeed, between 1851 and 1891, the column was headed 'rank, profession or occupation'. Detailed instruction on the terms to be used when completing this col-

---

[9] Higgs, op cit, p.85-6.   [10] Ibid, p.215-26.   [11] Ibid, p.72-4.

umn were given on householders schedules[12], but were frequently ignored. The returns were supposed to differentiate 'masters' from 'journeymen', but frequently householders and enumerators did not make the distinction. The unemployed were not separately distinguished until 1931, although some enumerators used terms such as 'out of work' or 'out of employment'. Students of occupations must confront the problem of inexactitude. Job titles are frequently vague, and may give no hint of the industry in which people were employed. The term 'labourer', for example, was frequently used without indicating the relevant industry. It was not until 1911 that a question was asked to elicit this information. Some terms meant different things in different places. A 'bank manager' for example, could be the superintendent at a mine's pithead, or he could be a financial expert.

Many occupational terms used in the nineteenth century are now obsolete. There are a number of dictionaries which define such terms:

* CULLING, JOYCE. *Occupations: a preliminary list.* 2nd ed. F.F.H.S., 1999.
* TWINING, ANDREW, & TWINING, SANDRA. *Dictionary of old trades and occupations.* Twinings Secretarial, 1993.
* WATERS, C. *A dictionary of old trades, titles and occupations.* Rev. ed. Countryside Books, 2002.

Despite these difficulties, the census enumerators' books have a great deal to offer to both family and local historians. They offer a comprehensive survey of Victorian society, unrivalled in scope. The information they provide is in a standardized format, which is much easier to analyse than most other historical sources.

Census Webpages

There are many websites offering census databases covering the whole country. Most of these (not all) require you to pay a fee for consultation. Before you do, you need (a) to understand what information they are likely to provide, and (b) know what alternatives there are that might be free.

Numerous web pages offer introductions to the census for family historians. Most do not offer any more information than is provided here. TNA has a research guide at:

* Census Returns
  www.nationalarchives.gov.uk/catalogue/RdLeaflet.asp?sLeafletID=326

Gateway Sites

A variety of general census websites are linked to by:

* England and Wales: Census
  www.genuki.org.uk/big/eng/Census.html
  There are many webpages offering census transcripts and indexes,

---

[12] These can be read at **www.histpop.org** (click 'TNA enumerators' books').

sometimes for the whole country, but more frequently for specific counties and parishes, and for specific census years. Some of the more important local sites are listed below, p. 39-43. Others can be found by using gateway sites. A number of these are devoted specifically to census material. I have excluded from this list a number of sites which are primarily intended to promote commercial sites.

- Census Finder: a Directory of Free Census Records
  www.censusfinder.com
  This site is international in scope
- British Census Indexes, Transcripts and Images Available Online or on CD
  www.mit.edu/~dfm/genealogy/census-chart.html
- Census Online: Your Guide to Online Census Records
  www.census-online.com
  International in scope
- Census Sites
  www.mick-gray.co.uk/census_sites.htm
- UK Census Online
  freepages.genealogy.rootsweb.ancestry.com/~babznz/ukcensus.html

The most useful census websites are listed in:

- RAYMOND, STUART A. *Family History on the Web: an internet directory for England and Wales.* 5th ed. Family History Partnership, 2008.

Internet Census Databases
A number of English websites offer databases with national coverage for particular census years. With the exception of 1881, these are mostly pay to view sites. The major exception to this rule is FreeCen **freecen.rootsweb.com**, which aims to provide free indexes and transcripts to all nineteenth century census returns (except 1881). It is far from being complete.

There are many other sites offering free county-wide or local data, as noted above. If you do not want to spend more money than you must, check the information these sites hold before you use commercial sites. Alternatively, visit your local record office or public library. Libraries sometimes offer free access to commercial sites. Free access to commercial sites is also available on site at TNA (although you will have to pay for any printouts you require).

Commercial sites generally offer a search facility (an index) which leads you to a transcript of the original record. Most will charge you to view this transcript, and make a further charge if you want to view the original image (which you really ought to do).

Family historians will usually wish to search for a particular surname. All the databases permit this to be done. Local historians, however, are more likely to search for the return for a particular place.

Not all databases permit such searches. Where this cannot be done, it may nevertheless be possible to find the return by searching for a particular person who is known to have lived in the place sought.

The following list of national databases is in alphabetical order, and attempts to indicate the pricing structure. Unfortunately, the pricing structure is not always clear. Some hosts do not tell their customers how much they are going to be charged until they have actually completed a search and are asked to pay for the results. Few sites set out full details of all their prices on one webpage. In some cases pricing structures are quite complicated, and unclear. Hosts often proclaim that searching is 'free' - but charge you to see the results of the search.

Such practices are annoying to those of us who want to know how much we will have to pay before we begin searching. Those sites which try to hide their costs obviously do not deserve to be used. The details of prices given below are taken from database websites.

Sites generally offer either a subscription service, with unlimited viewings, or a pay per view service, where you can see a specified number of results. Some offer both. The information on pricing noted below was current in November 2008. Prices are, of course, liable to change without notice.

- The 1901 Census for England & Wales
  www.1901censusonline.com
  Despite the name of the site, you can search all censuses, 1841-1901, here. Searching the index is free, but in order to view transcribed data you must pay 50 credits for an individual, plus 50 credits for a list of all other people in that person's household. Viewing a digital image of the census page (which is what you really need) costs 75 credits. 500 credits costs £5.00
- 1911 Census
  www.1911census.co.uk
- 192.com
  www.192.com/Genealogy
  This site has the 1861 census, plus civil registration indexes. It charges 1 credit for each transcript viewed, plus 1 credit for each image, but will not tell you how much a credit costs unless you register. The site also has indexes to the civil registers.
- Ancestry
  www.ancestry.co.uk
  This site has an extraordinarily wide range of databases, including all census returns, 1841-1911 (Scotland included), indexes to the civil registers, and much much more. But don't believe all the hype on the site! There are a range of payment options; for example, a monthly subscription to UK databases costs £10.95. An annual subscription would be £83.40. Twelve record views cost £6.95.

- British Origins
  www.britishorigins.com
  This site has census returns for 1841, 1861 and 1871. It also has a good range of other databases, including marriage registers, burial records, wills, passenger lists, militia, court and apprentice records. These databases mostly relate to material held by the Society of Genealogists. A subscription for 72 hours costs £6.50. A month costs £8.95.
- Family History Online
  www.familyhistoryonline.co.uk
  Numerous census indexes and transcripts compiled by family history societies are available on this site, which also has a good range of baptism, marriage and burial indexes, monumental inscriptions, and other sources. It was established by the Federation of Family History Societies, but is now run by Find My Past (see below). The cost of search results varies, depending on the database. Credits have to be purchased; they are available on-line in units of £5, £10, £20 and £50. If you do not like paying online, credits can also be purchased through a number of family history societies and other organizations.
- Family Relatives
  www.familyrelatives.com
  The census for 1841-91 is currently (November 2008) being tested, and will be available on this site in due course. Costs have not yet been indicated, but charges for other databases hosted are competitive.
- Family Search: Census Records
  www.familysearch.org
  Click on 'search' and 'census' for access to a full transcript (not digitised images) and index of the 1881 census, including Scotland. This is a free site, which gives access to the census microfilms of the Latter Day Saints (available through their worldwide network of Family History Centres, listed on the website). It is replicated on several of the sites listed here. It is also available on fiche, and many libraries and record offices have the fiche version.
- Find My Past
  www.findmypast.com
  All censuses are available on this site, including 1911, although for 1881 only transcripts, not the original returns, are available. Find My Past hosts a good range of other databases, including indexes to the civil registers, and records relating to migration, the military, and occupations. It is possible to take out a subscription, or to pay per view. 60 units cost £6.95, 280 cost £24.95. A census image costs 3 units; prices for other databases vary. The cheapest subscription including the census is for 12 months, and costs £64.95.

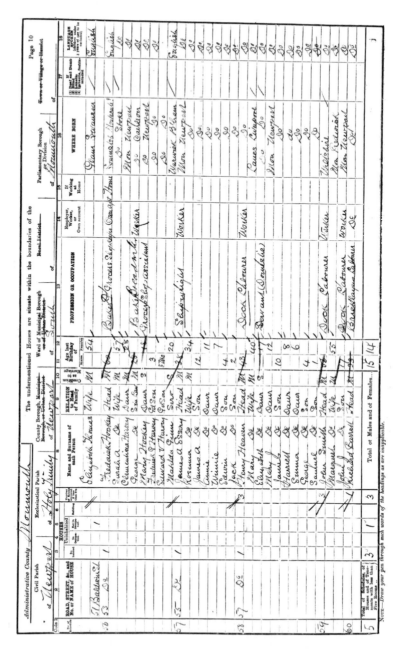

Figure 6. TNA RG13/4958, f.169. Census return, 1901, for Newport. The folio number is on the next page. See p. 46-8 for a discussion of the Hockey family entry

- FreeCen: UK Census Online
  freecen.rootsweb.com
  The FreeCen project is attempting to provide free indexes and transcripts of all nineteenth-century census returns (except 1881). It is far from complete, but is worth checking. Cornish censuses, for example, are almost complete. The database is, of course, only a transcript, and you may want to consult digitised images (or microfilm) of the original returns. Find the return you require here first, then use the information given to find the digitised image you need on a commercial database. If you have to consult several pages before you find the right one, this procedure may be cheaper.
- The Genealogist
  www.thegenealogist.co.uk
  All censuses, 1841 to 1901, are on this site. Digitised images are currently being added to the 1881 pages. The site also has civil registration indexes, nonconformist registers, and a number of other databases. Subcriptions cost from £4.66 per month. It is also possible to pay as you go, but costs are not clearly stated.

Census CDs
Many census returns are available on CD. These are particularly useful for local historians, who may want to browse returns for several parishes before selecting one for detailed study. Usually CDs contain digitised images of the original returns. Occasionally the returns have been transcribed. When purchasing CDs, alway check whether they are digitised images or transcripts, and whether they are indexed. Digitised images are always preferable to transcripts, as copying inevitably results in errors - which means that, sooner or later, you will need to consult a digitised image or microfilm. If a CD does not contain an index, you may spend a lot of time searching. Also, be aware that some census CDs merely contain indexes, and not the returns themselves.

Most CD publishers issue sets of CDs covering whole counties. Some bundle together all the censuses for a particular county. Occasionally, CDs for particular registration districts may be available separately.

CDs covering most counties and census years for England and Wales have been published. Those issued by family history societies (and some other publishers) are often available through:
- Genfair
  www.genfair.com
CDs from a variety of publishers are also available from:
- The Parish Chest
  www.parishchest.com

There are many CD publishers, far too many to list here. Most of them only cover one or two counties. Major publishers include:
- British Data Archive
  www.britishdataarchive.com
- Onegene
  www.onegene.co.uk

The 1851 and 1891 censuses for a number of counties are available from:
- My Censuses
  www.mycensuses.com

To identify other publishers, use a search engine such as Google **www.google.co.uk**, combining the terms 'census', 'CD', and the name of the county you are interested in. Be aware that many census returns have been published by more than one CD publisher, and compare their prices. Be aware, too, that publishers may merge or close down. 'Archive CD Books' may serve as an example of a major CD publisher, which has recently closed its UK operations, although overseas sites remain open, for example:
- Archive CD Books USA
  www.archivecdbooksusa.com

Publishers frequently advertise CDs in magazines such as *Family tree magazine, Ancestors, Family history monthly,* and *Your family tree.*

Microfiche & Microfilm
The advent of digitised images on census websites and CDs means that most researchers do not need to use the older technology of fiche and film. The internet and CDs are much easier to search than microfilm, although they may be more expensive. Microfilm is, however, still available in most local studies libraries and record offices, and in some family history society research centres. Most institutions will only have fiche or film for the areas they cover (some may not have bothered to acquire them for 1901). The Family History Library of the Latter Day Saints holds a full set of microfilm, which can be borrowed through their network of Family History Centres. Visit **www.familysearch.org** for details. Public libraries which hold census microfilms are listed at:
- Familia
  www.familia.org.uk

See also:
- GIBSON, JEREMY. *Census returns 1841-91 in microform: a directory to local holdings in Great Britain; Channel Islands; Isle of Man.* 6th ed. F.F.H.S., 1994.

If cost is a consideration, start by using one of the free internet databases mentioned above. Then check your search results against a microfilm, if you have free access to one. That will save the cost of using a commercial database - although it may take much longer.

Many libraries and record offices also have the fiche version of the 1881 census published by the Latter Day Saints. This was the first census to be fully transcribed, as a result of a cooperative venture between the Latter Day Saints and the Federation of Family History Societies. As already noted, this transcript is also available on the internet. The fiche version has a 'surname index', a 'birthplace index', a 'census place index', and an 'as enumerated' index (which is not really an index). It also has a number of useful supplementary fiche, including a 'list of institutions', and a 'list of vessels/ships'. A guide to the fiche version of the index is available at:

- 1881 British Census Indexes
  www.familysearch.org
  (click on 'search', 'research helps', and 'E', then scroll down)

Recording the Source of your Information
Despite the availability of digitised images on the internet and CD, it is still a good idea to include TNA references when recording the results of your searches. Then you will be able to check your results again, regardless of which website or other media you use.

TNA assigns a class reference to every series of documents in its possession. For the census, these references are:

1841 & 1851 HO 107	1891 RG 12
1861 RG 9	1901 RG 13
1871 RG 10	1911 RG 14 (see also RG 78)
1881 RG 11	

Census enumerators' books are stored in folders and boxes. Several books are in each folder, and several folders in each box. Piece numbers are assigned either to the box, or to the folder, depending on the census year. Each book has its own internal page numbering. There are also folio numbers which cover the whole 'piece'. These are stamped consecutively on the top right hand corner of every right-hand page, beginning with the first page of the first book in each folder (for 1841 and 1861-1901) or box (for 1851), and ending with the last page of the last book in that folder or box. For example, the 1851 return for Launcells, Cornwall, may be cited as HO 107/1897, f.92-212. If there are many pages in a 'piece', then it may be desirable to add page numbers to your reference.

If you are using a digitised image online, and the host does not give you the piece number, then you can find it by using TNA's search engine at **www.nationalarchives.gov.uk/search**. Piece numbers are also noted in:

- ROSIER, M.E.B. *Index to census registration districts, 1841-1891*. 6th ed. The author, 1999.

Place Name Indexes

Users of microfiche and microfilm will need to consult place name and street indexes in order to locate entries in the census. Institutions which hold film should hold copies of the relevant indexes; a full set (other than locally produced indexes) is held by TNA. There is a *Placename index*, and a *Reference book*, for each census year. The 1841 *Placename index* gives you a page number in the 1841 *Reference book*, which list the places covered by particular pieces, and gives you the piece numbers. You will need these numbers to find the correct films.

For 1851 and subsequent census years, the procedure is different. The place name index gives you the number of the registration district covering the place you wish to research. You must then consult the Reference book, to locate the registration district using that number (which is the district number, not a page number). The entry lists the sub-districts and parishes included in the registration district, giving the piece numbers.

If you are following a lead from a civil registration certificate, that certificate will tell you the relevant registration district. You will therefore only need to consult the reference book to identify piece numbers.

Street Indexes

If you are searching for a particular street in London or other towns with a population exceeding 40,000, and using microfilm, you will need to consult a street index. These give the piece and folio numbers that you will need in order to find the correct microfilm. For London especially, street names were continually being changed. Alterations are noted in:

- *London County Council list of streets & places within the administrative County of London [& City of London] shewing localities, postal districts, parishes, metropolitan boroughs, electoral divisions, ordnance & municipal map references, together with the alterations in street nomenclature & numbering since 1856.* London County Council, [1912]

A variety of other helps to locating particular places are listed by Lumas[13]. See also:

- England: How to Use Census Street Indexes
  www.familysearch.org/eng/default.asp
  (Click on, 'research helps', 'guidance', and scroll down)

Surname Indexes

Innumerable census indexes were compiled by family history societies and others in the last decades of the twentieth century. These are very useful for locating specific entries if you are using the census on microfiche or microfilm. They are redundant if you are using the internet, or CDs which have their own indexes.

---

[13] Lumas, op cit, p. 21-30.

Census indexes are listed in a number of places. Most are listed in:

- PERKINS, JOHN P. *Current Publications on microfiche by Member Societies.* 5th ed. 2002.
- HAMPSON, ELIZABETH. *Current Publications by Member Societies.* 10th ed. 1999.

The only comprehensive listing of both published and unpublished indexes is:

- GIBSON, JEREMY, & HAMPSON, ELIZABETH. *Marriage and census indexes for family historians.* 7th ed. F.F.H.S., 1998.

Most indexes were prepared before these books were published, so they are still useful despite their age. Published indexes can also be found by using the library catalogue of the Society of Genealogists, which has a comprehensive collection:

- Sogcat
  www.sog.org.uk
  (click on title)

Both published and unpublished indexes can be identified on the websites of family history societies. For a list of these, visit:

- Family History and Genealogy Societies
  www.genuki.org.uk/Societies

County Websites and Handbooks

In addition to the major national sites listed above, there are numerous local webpages providing information about the census. A small number of handbooks listing resources for particular counties are also available. Some of the more important websites, and the county handbooks, are listed below. Reference is also made to two CDs.

Many websites provide county-wide transcripts and indexes, most of them free. Others provide useful information about the availability of census information. FreeCen's county pages **freecen.rootsweb.com** are not listed here, nor are the many county indexes on Family History Online **www.familyhistoryonline.co.uk**. Much information is also available on Genuki's county pages **www.genuki.org.uk**.

Berkshire

- 1851 Berkshire Census Surname Index
  www.berksfhs.org.uk/
  Census1851surnames_files/Census1851surnames.htm
- Berkshire 1871 Census Transcription Project Progress
  www.berksfhs.org.uk/projects/
  Berkshire1871CensusProjectProgress.htm

Cambridgeshire

- Cambridgeshire 1841 Census Index
  www.cfhs.org.uk/1841Index
- Cambridgeshire 1851 Census Index
  www.cfhs.org.uk/1851Index
- Cambridgeshire 1861 census Index
  www.cfhs.org.uk/1861Index

Derbyshire

- South Derbyshire Genealogy Pages
  freepages.genealogy.rootsweb.com/~brett/sdindex.htm
  Includes many census transcripts for Repton & Gresley Hundred

Devon

- Searching the L.D.S. 1851 Devon Census CD-Rom
  genuki.cs.ncl.ac.uk/DEV/Census1851searching.html

Co. Durham

- Transcripts of the 1841, 1861, 1871 and 1891 Census Returns covering areas of Co. Durham and Northumberland
  www.genuki.bpears.org.uk/CenTrans.html
  List of transcripts and indexes for parishes and townships, *etc.*
- Durham Records Online
  www.durhamrecordsonline.com
  Includes index to various census transcripts. Pay per view site.

Essex see *London & Middlesex*

Hampshire

- Hampshire Family History Census Returns
  website.lineone.net/~hantshistory/census.html
  Gateway
- ALLEN, MARK, & JONES, TIM BEAUMONT. *The 1871 census of Winchester.* CD. Winchester historical databases. University of Winchester, 2006. Includes detailed discussion.

Kent

A guide to census returns for Kent is provided by:
- WRIGHT, DAVID. *The Kentish census returns 1801-1901: origins, location, registration districts and indexes.* 2003. Available from the author at
  www.davideastkent.canterhill.co.uk/index.htm

Kent census indexing has been piecemeal. There are many indexes, both published and unpublished. A detailed listing is provided by:
- Kent Census: Index Coverage in maps 1841-1901
  www.archersoftware.co.uk/census

If you prefer your information in book format, then consult:
- RICKARD, GILLIAN. *Kent Census Surname Indexes 1801-1901*. 2005. (available from 'Kent Family History Research' www.kentgen.com/publications.htm#surname)

Lancashire
- 1891 Liverpool Census www.liverpool-genealogy.org.uk/Information/1891Census.htm

Lincolnshire
- Lincolnshire Census www.genuki.org.uk/big/eng/LIN/census.html Detailed introduction; many links
- Parkinson Page: Census www.wparkinson.com/1861.htm Transcription of the 1861 census for villages S.W. of Lincoln
- Sedgebrook Inhabitants of Yesteryear myweb.tiscali.co.uk/hampson Transcriptions of a village's census returns for 1841, 1851, 1861, 1871, 1891 and 1901, *etc.*

London & Middlesex
- London Census Surname Indexes homepage.ntlworld.com/hitch/gendocs/loncen.html List of published indexes available

Some census indexes for Middlesex, Essex, Kent and Surrey are listed in:
- GIBSON, JEREMY, & CREATON, HEATHER. *Lists of Londoners*. 3rd ed. F.F.H.S., 1999.

Norfolk
- Norfolk Transcription Archive www.genealogy.doun.org/transcriptions Includes census transcripts for many parishes and dates

- Norfolk Census Information and List of Villages with Names Index for the 1891 Census apling.freeservers.com/CensusInfo.htm

Northamptonshire
- Northamptonshire 1841 Census Full Transcription www.northants1841.fsnet.co.uk

Somerset
- Census Transcriptions
  freepages.genealogy.rootsweb.ancestry.com/
  ~sarahhawkins/census_transcriptions.htm
  Collection of miscellaneous Somerset transcripts
- The Bath and Surrounding Area 1841 Census
  www.geocities.com/chris_gh_walker/geneology/bathcensus1841.html
  Offline database

Staffordshire
- 1861 Census
  www.griffs4bears.co.uk/census/home.html
  For Dudley & Stourbridge
- Walsall Council: Local Census Indexes
  www.walsall.gov.uk/index/
  leisure_and_culture/localhistorycentre/local_census_indexes.htm
  Various census indexes for Walsall district.

Suffolk
For detailed information on published and unpublished indexes, see:
- BOURNE, SUSAN. *Indexes for the Suffolk family historian*. 2nd ed. The author, 1998.

Surrey see also *London & Middlesex*
There are two useful guides to the Surrey census:
- *Guide to the Surrey censuses of 1841, 1851 and 1861*. Research Aids **5**.
  7th ed. West Surrey Family History Society, 2007.
- *Guide to the Surrey censuses 1871, 1881, 1891 & 1901*. Research Aids **9**.
  3rd ed. West Surrey Family History Society, 2007.
The only online database for Surrey worth mention is:
- The Kingston Life Cycles Database
  localhistory.kingston.ac.uk/database/LocalHistoryForm.asp
  Database for Kingston on Thames, 1851-91 (also includes marriage & burial registers)

Wiltshire
- Nimrod Research
  www.nimrodindex.co.uk
  Details of an off-line index to the Wiltshire 1851 census

WALES
- Welsh Census Returns 1851, 1891: Surname Index Census Returns
  www.jewishgen.org/databases/UK/walescen.htm
  Index of Jews in the census

Anglesey
- Search Amlwch Census Databases
  www.parysmountain.co.uk
  Click on 'Amlwch genealogy' and 'select a database subject'. Various databases for Amlwch and surrounding area.

Pembrokeshire
- CenQuest: Census Research Wales
  www.cenquest.co.uk
  Index to the Pembrokeshire Census for 1871 (partial) and 1891; also bordering parts of Cardiganshire and Carmarthenshire. Pay per view database.

CHANNEL ISLANDS
The census in the Channel Islands were administered with the English census from 1821. Returns are available on a number of the databases listed above (p. 32-5), including Ancestry.com and (for 1881) Family Search. See also
- 1841 Census Channel Islands
  www.members.shaw.ca/jerseymaid

IRELAND
Censuses in Ireland were taken in 1813, and then every ten years between 1821 and 1911. Unfortunately, most returns have been lost due to fire or government vandalism. No manuscript returns survive for 1861, 1871, 1881 and 1891. The Irish National Archives do hold some returns for 1821, 1831, 1841 and 1851, covering parts of counties Antrim, Cavan, Cork, Fermanagh, Galway, King's County (Offaly), Londonderry (Derry), Meath and Waterford. A listing of all substantial surviving returns is provided by:
- ROYLE, S.A. 'Irish manuscript census returns: a neglected source of information', *Irish geography*, **11**, p.118-25. For the supposed 1831 returns, see the correction in **14**, 1981, p.142.

The Irish National Archives also hold the returns for 1901 and 1911. These are arranged by townland in rural areas, by street in urban areas. The returns for each townland or street consist of:

1. Householders' schedules (forms A), completed by the head of each household, giving the name, age, sex, relationship to head of the household, religion, occupation, marital status, and county or country of birth, of each resident member of the household. The returns also indicate whether people were able to read and write, whether they spoke Irish, and whether they were deaf, dumb, blind, an idiot, an imbecile, or a lunatic. There are also house and building returns (forms B1), and returns of out-offices and farm-steadings (forms B2)

2. Enumerators schedules (forms N), which summarise the household-ers' schedules. In addition to the enumerators' abstracts, there are also a range of institutional and shipping returns, similar (although not identical) to those found in England.

Digitisation of these schedules is currently in progress, in a joint project of the Irish National Archives, and Library and Archives Canada. The Dublin census 1911 has just been launched:

* Census of Ireland: Dublin 1911
  www.census.nationalarchives.ie

Further information on the Irish National Archives holdings of census records is given in:

* National Archives of Ireland: Census Returns: 1901 and 1911 Census Digitisation Project
  www.nationalarchives.ie/genealogy/censusrtns.html

The Public Record Office of Northern Ireland holds microfilm copies of the 1901 and 1911 censuses for its territory. These are described in:

* Your Family Tree Series 2: 1901 census
  www.proni.gov.uk/your_family_tree_series_-_02_-_1901_census.pdf

For an introduction to the Irish census, see:

* Irish Ancestors: Census Records
  scripts.ireland.com/ancestor/browse/records/census

A detailed guide for local historians is provided by:

* CRAWFORD, E.M. *Counting the people: a survey of the Irish censuses, 1813-1911*. Four Courts Press, 2003.

There are also many websites offering transcripts of surviving fragments from Irish censuses. The gateways listed above (p. 31) include many links to Irish sites. See also:

* Actual Censuses
  www.rootsweb.com/~fianna/guide/cen1.html
* Online Irish Census Indexes & Records: Ireland Census Records by County: a genealogy guide
  www.genealogybranches.com/irishcensus.html

A variety of local census websites for Ireland are listed in:

* RAYMOND, STUART A. *Irish family history on the web: a directory*. 3rd ed. Family History Partnership, 2007.

ISLE OF MAN

The census on the Isle of Man, from 1821, was administered with the English and Welsh censuses. The 1901 census for the island asked whether Manx was spoken. All other questions were identical to those asked in England.

A duplicate copy of the returns was made for 1851, 1861, and 1871. These duplicates are held in the Manx Museum, where they can be seen on microfilm. Returns held by TNA are available on Ancestry.com,

Family Search (for 1881), and some of the other database websites listed above (p. 32-5). A useful introduction to Isle of Man censuses is provided by:

- Census Records
  www.isle-of-an.com/manxnotebook/famhist/genealgy/census.htm
  For 1871, visit:
- The 1871 Isle of Man census
  www.familyhistory101.com/r
  esearch-census/census_isleofman_1871.html

SCOTLAND

Since 1861, the Scottish census has been administered by the General Register Office for Scotland, who still hold the original returns. Like those in England, they can only be consulted by using digitised images or microfiche. There are some minor differences from the English returns. From 1861, the Scottish census identified employers, and indicated how many people they employed. They indicated how many rooms occupied by a family had windows, and, from 1891, whether people spoke Gaelic. And they provide a space for 'remarks of the minister of the parish'.[14] Mostly, these remarks affirm the accuracy of the information given.

The essential website for the Scottish census is:

- Scotlands People
  www.scotlandspeople.gov.uk

This has digitised images of all censuses, 1841-71 and 1891-1901, together with very detailed introductions to each census (showing examples of returns for every census year). For 1881, it has a copy of the transcript and index from the Family Search site. The returns will presumably be digitised eventually. The 1911 return will be added in 2011. Scotlands People is a pay per view site. £6 purchases 30 'page credits'.

Returns are also available on Ancestry **www.ancestry.co.uk,** and (for 1881) on Family Search **www.familysearch.org**. You may prefer to begin by checking FreeCen, which is working towards a free transcription and index of all Scottish censuses:

- FreeCen Scotland Website
  www.freewebs.com/mmjeffery/index.htm
  Scroll down to see what is currently available

The gateways listed above (p. 30-31) include links to a variety of other Scottish sites. See also:

- Scotland: Census
  www.genuki.org.uk/big/sct/Census.html

---

[14] See JONES, CHRISTINE. 'The fitness of the person employed: comments in the Scottish census enumerators books', *Local population studies* **79**, 2007, p.75-80.

A wide variety of Scottish census websites (mainly of local interest) are listed in:

- RAYMOND, STUART A. *Scottish family history on the web: a directory*. 2nd ed. F.F.H.S., 2005.

Case Study 1. The Hockey Family[15]

Ada Hockey was 26 in 1901, when Ancestry's on-line census return records that she lived at 86, Commercial Road, Newport, Monmouthshire. Her occupation was given as 'grocer and shopkeeper', and she was single. Two sisters, Mabel and Martha, lived with her, and helped to run the shop. According to the census, her neighbours were all shopkeepers; Commercial Road was one of the major shopping centres in the city.

What were three young ladies doing running a grocer's shop together, without any male help? We shall probably never know the precise circumstances, but it is probably relevant that Ada married Edmund Bennett later in 1901. The Bennetts continued to run the business together for many years. The background is provided by consulting the 1891 census. It reveals Ada, Martha, and Mabel living with their father, Frederick Hockey, who was then a 'baker and grocer'. He lived with his wife Sarah and their seven children, at 27, Baldwin Street, Newport. He carried on his business in a working class district. His neighbours were dock labourers. He had evidently helped his daughters establish their own shop.

Returning to the 1901 census, Frederick and Sarah can be found still living in Baldwin Street, but at No 53. Either the family had moved down the street, or the street had been re-numbered. Two daughters were still living at home, but one of them, Clementina, was married. Her husband, George Harvey, and their two young children, were also living with the in-laws. Ada, Martha, and Mabel had perhaps moved out in order to make room for George, who was described as 'baker breadmkr'. Frederick was still carrying on his business, but needed George to help him. George probably baked for Ada's shop as well as Frederick's. Frederick's youngest daughter, Mary, aged 18, also helped in the shop.

The 1901 return shows that Frederick had been born in Montacute, Somerset, and that he was aged 60. Sarah's birthplace was given simply as 'Stoke', Somerset. She was then 57. Earlier censuses gave different birthplace information. Both Frederick and Sarah were said to have been born in 'Somerset' in the 1881 and 1891 returns. No other information was given. In 1871, Frederick was said to have been born at Odcombe (which borders Montacute). Sarah was said to have been born in Rodney Stoke.

---

[15]   See figures 3-6 (p. 16, 19, 20 and 34) for Hockey family entries in the censuses of 1841, 1871, 1881 and 1901.

The 1881 census return was difficult to find. The transcribers of the database at **www.familysearch.org** had mistranscribed 'Hockey' as 'Hokey' (see p. 20). Little had changed in the years between 1881 and 1891, except that the children had grown up. In 1881, only Henry John, Frederick's oldest child, had been old enough to be described as a 'bakers asst'. He was then 15. Frederick himself was described as a 'master baker Employ 1 Man 2 Boys'. Did he branch out into the grocery business in the 1880s, or was the term 'baker' being used to include trading as a grocer?

The 1871 return shows that the family had not moved, but there were only three children, aged 5, 3, and 8 months. Frederick was described simply as a baker. Frederick had evidently married Sarah at some point during the 1860s. In the 1861 census, he can be found living with his parents, Parmenas and Eliza at 54, Dolphin Street, Newport. Parmenas was a 'baker and publican'; Frederick was a baker. The father was born in Montacute, the son in Odcombe. Eliza's birthplace was given as 'Kingtinghull', Somerset. The enumerator's spelling is incorrect, and confusion was worse confounded by the indexer, who transcribed this place as 'Kinglinbone'. Neither the enumerator nor the indexer correctly identified this place.

A search for Eliza in the 1871 census shows that she was a widow living at 68, Dolphin Street, Newport. The return clarified the fact that she was actually born in Tintinhull. She had evidently not continued as a publican when her husband died, and it is likely that she had moved down the street (although it is also possible that the houses in her street had been re-numbered). The most useful feature of this return, from the family historian's point of view, is that Eliza was living with various relatives. Her son John had followed in his father's footsteps and become a baker. Also present was her sister, Mary Beaton, a dressmaker, and her daughter, also Mary. The elder Mary was described as 'unmarried', so her daughter must have been illegitimate. More important from the family historian's point of view, is that Eliza's maiden name must also have been Beaton.

The 1851 return also states that Eliza was born in Tintinhull. At that date, the family was living at 53, Dolphin Street. One neighbour was a master mariner, the other a butcher's journeyman. Parmenas was described as a 'Baker Master', and his son James, aged 13, was a 'baker journeyman'. There is no mention of the licenced trades. There were five children altogether, three sons and two daughters.

The 1841 census finds the family in Odcombe. Frederick was three months old. His two siblings were toddlers. This census gives no birthplace information. Nor does it indicate relationships, although, in the case of the Hockeys, we know these from later censuses. The interesting feature of this return is that Parmenas was described as a 'sailcloth manufacturer'. This was a declining industry. The long peace after 1815 considerably reduced the Royal Navy's demand for sailcloth. It is not surprising that Parmenas decided to emigrate across the Bristol Channel. He was not alone. Newport was rapidly industrializing, and had plenty of opportunities for those prepared to work. Any local historian researching the history of Somerset parishes, or of Newport, has to take into account the numerous Somersetians who can be found in nineteenth century census returns for Newport.

The evidence presented above shows how much information can be derived from the census. There are, of course, pitfalls. It has been shown that neither census enumerators, nor indexers, can be entirely trusted. The information they provide must always be viewed critically.

Census information contains many clues that may lead to further information. The census can be used as a gateway to information that can be found in other sources. It gives the names and ages of many family members. That information can be used to search for entries in both parish and civil registers. Civil and parish registers could be checked for the marriages and baptisms of Frederick and Sarah's parents and children. For example, Parmenas's father, Luke, can be found in the parish register, and can therefore be identified in the Odcombe 1841 census, not far from his son's residence. Other relatives could also be traced.

It is likely that more information about Frederick and Ada's grocery business could be found in trade directories. They probably advertised in local newspapers, which could be searched. Parmenas's publican's licence may be traceable. It is possible that Mary Beaton had to apply for poor relief when her illegitimate daughter was born. Records might sur-

Figure 7. The Hockey Family, late 1880s.

vive amongst Poor Law Union records. Parish records (not just the registers) in Odcombe and Montacute could also be searched for information about the early nineteenth century family, as could the estate records of local landlords. Does a lease of Parmenas's cottage survive?

A great deal can be discovered by combining census evidence with information from parish and civil registers, trade directories, poor law records, estate records, and other sources (some of which will be dealt with in future volumes of this series).

Case Study 2: The Family of Theophilus Ratcliffe

Theophilus Ratcliffe was a bathchairman aged 44 when he was recorded in the Brighton 1891 census. He lived at 10, Norfolk Street, with his wife Penny, aged 84(!), and his children Edward P (12), and Josephine R (11). Penny's age is obviously incorrect; ten years earlier, in 1881, she was only 32. The enumerator wrote '8' when he meant '4'.

The 1881 census differs in a number of other ways from its 1891 successor. The couple had moved to no 5, Norfolk Street. We know that they had moved, rather than had their house re-numbered, because the occupants of no. 4 next door had not changed in the intervening ten years. Theophilus's occupation was recorded in 1881 as 'flyman'. In 1891, he was said to have been born in Lower Compton; the 1881 census records his birthplace as Staffordshire. Neither is correct. The 1861 and 1871 censuses (see below) show that he was born in Long Compton, Warwickshire.

Both censuses state that Penny was born in Lindfield, Sussex (although in 1881 this is mis-spelt as 'Linfield'). This can be confirmed by consulting their marriage certificate, which records that they were married at Lindfield on 29th October, 1876. Theophilus was then living in Marylebone, and working as a dealer. The certificate states that his father was William, a gardener.

Theophilus's children in 1881 were Robert P, aged 2 yrs and 9 months, described as a 'scholar' (he must have been precocious!), and Josephen, aged 1 year, both born in Brighton. Was Robert the same child as Edward, who appeared in the 1891 census? The answer is not apparent in the census. No record of his birth certificate has been found. Recourse must be had to his marriage certificate, dated 20th January, 1899, which names him as 'Edward Robert Percy'. He was a footman, living in Kensington, but he married a Sussex girl. The 1901 census shows him as a butler living in London, working for Arthur Bristowe, whilst his wife and daughter were living in Hove.

Edward's marriage certificate states that his father, described as a coachman, was dead. A search for his death certificate reveals that he died accidentally in 1898, and that a coroner's inquest was held. The *Westminster & Pimlico News* gave a full account of the inquest. Theophilus's death was caused by his falling downstairs whilst drunk.

49

The report stated that his son 'John Radcliffe' had identified the body. No such son has been identified in the census, although we do know from earlier censuses that Theophilus had a brother John. The reporter probably made an error.

Theophilus's earlier life can also be traced in the census. In 1871, he was aged 22, and working as a groom in Tanworth, Warwickshire. He was the servant of Mary Lowe, a landowner. This ties in with his later career as a flyman in 1881, a bathchairman in 1891, a stablehand when he died, and a coachman according to his son's marriage certificate. It may be that the Lowe family found him a place in London, and then in Brighton. A search could be made for Lowe family and estate papers, which may throw more light on Theophilus. In 1861, he was aged 10, living at home in Long Compton with his father William, who was described as a gardener. As noted above, that was also his employment in 1876.

William and his wife Hannah had five children living at home in 1861. The eldest, James (20), was a mason's labourer, and the next eldest, Thomas (15), a gardener like his father. Theophilus's other brothers were John Orlando (8), perhaps the 'son' who identified Theophilus's body in 1898, and Israel (6). There was also a daughter, Rosehannah. In 1881, Israel, then aged 25, was living with his widowed mother, still in Long Compton.

In 1851, there were more divergences. The family was still living in Long Compton, but their name was spelt 'Ratliffe'. Children were Richard, aged 14, who had left home by 1861, James (10), Thomas (6), Rosehannah (3), and Theophilus (aged 1).

In 1841, there were yet more divergences. Hannah Ratcliff was aged 25, and was described as 'Ind', that is, independent. William was absent from home, perhaps travelling to help with the harvest. The 1841 census was taken in June, and was moved to the end of March in 1851 in order to avoid the problems caused by itinerants moving around the country later in the year. Children included William (8), Ann (8), Richard (5), Eleanor (3), and James (9 months). William and Ann had left home by 1851. Eleanor was working in nearby Weston House.

William, Theophilus, and Edward Ratcliffe probably worked for landowners. Their occupations - gardener, bathchairman, butler - demonstrate that. These were occupations that catered for the needs of the landed gentry and the wealthy. We know that Theophilus was a groom to the Lowe family in 1871. It is possible that papers relating to the Lowe family survive in record offices; if so, they might reveal more information about Theophilus. The papers of the Bristowe family, if they can be found, may contain information relating to Edward. The civil registers might also reveal information about his siblings and his children. It should also be possible to trace his siblings through the census.

Index